Publish Your Book on Amazon for Free
How to Self-Publish Without Paying a Dime

Eddie Snipes

A book by:
Eddie Snipes

Copyright © 2015 by Eddie Snipes and
Exchanged Life Discipleship

http://www.exchangedlife.com

ISBN: 978-1515161752

D0681736

Contact the author by visiting http://www.eddiesnipes.com or http://www.exchangedlife.com

Table of Contents

Introduction to Self-Publishing

The industry has changed. Most authors haven't caught on. Most publishers are desperately trying to reverse the trend. A lot of vanity presses are using unscrupulous practices to play off author ignorance, and they leach as much money as possible. The industry makes a lot of money off authors, and most writers are left with little or nothing to show for their work. But the tide is changing.

Thanks to Amazon, the industry is changing and authors now have the power over their own work. The old way was, spend years begging for someone to look at your manuscript in the hopes you'll get an offer, or spend thousands to have the book published by a vanity press. No longer are these our only options.

Some vanity presses are honorable, while others are not. Some very unchristian-like publishing houses claim to be ministry-minded solely for the purpose of bilking money out of trusting people. Unscrupulous business people are like politicians. They will become whatever you want them to become until they get from you what they want. It's your job to use discernment and find a company that fits your needs.

Who should publish on their own?

If you can follow instructions and don't mind tinkering, you should consider doing the work on your own. If you need an editor, you can hire this out for a reasonable price. With this book, you should be able to do everything but editing.

When it comes to cover design, you can download a template and build your own cover from scratch, or you can utilize online cover creator tools. Both can produce professional looking results, but the online tool has a few limitations, which we'll discuss later

It is very much possible to publish your book from start to finish without spending a penny. What's more, you can set the price on your book. Where vanity presses force you to overprice your books, with Amazon, you can set your ebook price for as little as 99 cents, and your print books at competitive prices in the market.

Why Amazon?

I'm amazed that no one has followed the lead of Amazon. They are running away with the market, and they are wooing independent authors. Amazon has provided many valuable tools for marketing books, and done more to help authors get to the market than any other retailer.

The second leading online retailer makes it difficult to self-publish. When I published my first book, I tried to get it listed on this retailer's site. They required the author to send only two books to their warehouse. If it sold, they would permit the author to send more. It took a minimum of six weeks for the book to show up online. Ebooks had to go through an accepted third party. It could not be listed directly on the site.

Smashwords.com has provided a good option for authors as well, though not as good as Amazon. I quit using Smashwords for a few reasons. One of the main reasons is because of book formatting. Their system requires authors go through a tedious 117 page style guide requirement for formatting the manuscript for what they call 'the meat grinder'. Once the manuscript is perfectly formatted, the meat grinder strips the file down to a generic text document that is compatible with all formats.

You have little control over how the final format appears, and sometimes it is very unprofessional looking. The last time I used it, it did not allow for footnotes, which I use heavily.

Because they are a distributor, payment takes longer than it does on Amazon. Once the feed is established with retailers such as Apple, Kobo, and Barnes and Noble, these retailers have to wait for their books to clear, then they send the price minus their fees and commissions to Smashwords, and then Smashwords takes their cut and passes the commission to the author. The commission is 60%, which is a good price. However, Amazon pays up to 70% commission.

One big show-stopper is that smashwords requires authors to list Smashwords as the publisher on both the title page and the copyright page. There is no option to list your own imprint as the publisher of record.

One of the motivating factors for switching to Amazon is volume. Out of my first 1500 books sold, all but three were from Amazon. Since smashwords and Amazon aren't friends, books have to be published twice. When I looked at the sales, .002% of my sales was outside of Amazon. Was it worth the time invested to sell three more books?

Add to this, if you sell your book exclusively on Amazon, you can put your book in the Amazon Select program. This gives you the option for doing a countdown promo, where the book is at a reduced price with a clock showing the time left in the promo. You can also use the free promo option, which is a great way to get your book listed on blogs and promo sites. This helps get the title noticed. Free promos have always generated more sales for my books.

Another benefit is the Kindle Lending Library. Amazon select books have the option to be added to the lending library, where prime members can download it for free. It's free for the reader, but pays you. Amazon has a large pool of money each quarter that is divided among its authors based on the number of loaned books. Some months the borrowed books revenue exceeds the commissions on sales.

The biggest benefit is ease of publishing. With the combination of the Kindle publishing tools, and the CreateSpace publishing tools, it has never been easier to publish a high-quality, professional-looking book. The author cost per book is a fraction of the cost of any vanity press I have seen. You can buy one book, or thousands of books. Since it is POD (print on demand), there is no need to do a full print run, which is costly for independent authors.

An author that needs 2-4,000 books at a time can still outsource their print files for a full print run, but for smaller orders, the POD option is cost effective.

Who Should Use a Vanity Press?

This book is not intended to disparage publishing companies that are making a living off providing relevant services with honorable business practices. Though I'll gladly disparage the industry as a whole. There are a few good vanity presses, and a lot of bad ones.

An author I know recently spent $12,000 to get her book published. This price included several hundred 'free copies'. The retail book price was $24.95, and the author price was 'discounted' to $12.95. This publishing house does not make money off selling author's books to the public market. They make money off selling inflated services and overpriced books to authors.

Another author spent thousands to get her book published, and the publishing company only provided print copies. In order to get it in an ebook format, they had to spend more money for these services. Though they paid for the book cover design, the contract gave all rights to the publishing house, and when they decided to leave the company, they had to redesign the cover in a way that wouldn't violate the copyright. Yet another author found out she no longer owned her manuscript. The fine print gave the manuscript copyright to the publishing house, so her book was forever stuck in an overpriced vanity press.

This is why research and due diligence is vital.

For most authors, a vanity press is not the best option. By vanity press, I am using the industry terminology that means a self-publishing press. It's the idea that people want to see their work in print, and because they pay for it, it's just vanity – i.e. like looking in the mirror to admire yourself.

It's not an accurate concept in most cases, but it's an identifier most people have heard. Though, the industry is changing. The industry itself seeks to exclude self-published authors, but the stigma is fading thanks to companies that have successfully provided a market for independent authors.

If you are not technical, you may be a candidate for a vanity press that has ethical business practices. Don't trust the company's website. Search Google to see how other authors have reported their experience with that company. A self-published book has to supply its own services, such as editing, formatting / typesetting, cover design, marketing, printing, and distribution. If you are someone who doesn't want to deal with the backend work of publishing, it might be worth it to hire a company to do this for you.

One thing to consider is contracting typesetting, editing, and cover design out individually. You can get quality work for a lot less cost than most vanity presses. But for some people, not dealing with the headache is worth the price.

Let me give a word of warning. It is my recommendation that you not hire a publicist, nor should you buy a marketing package. Most self-publishing houses have a 'deluxe' option that includes marketing. They will include a press release that goes to many book distribution companies, and retail chains. This option is worthless.

On the website of one of the largest book chains, the company explains how it selects books. This company carries a little less than 30,000 books in its system. Only 10-15,000 are in its stores. Since nearly a million titles are published each year, this chain takes the top 10% of books, based on established authors. It then has a selection process that filters out everything except the titles that are expected to bring in the most revenue. Very little consideration is given for up and coming authors, and these are only selected from recommendations of major publishing houses.

The bottom line is, your chances of getting in a brick and mortar store through press releases are ZERO. Through your own marketing, you might get your books into independent book stores, but it is extremely rare for a self-published author to get into a major retailer. I have never heard of a single example, but there may be an example out there somewhere. The closest example would be the book 'The Shack.' This began as a self-published book, but was picked up by a publishing house. It did not succeed because of vanity press marketing.

You are your best marketer. A publicist is rarely a better marketer than you are. When I published my first book, I decided to hire a publicist. I paid a decent sum based on the promises they gave. The publicist only did the things I was already doing. They set up a blog tour, but the blogs they reached out to were already on my radar. I had already gone down this road to set up blog interviews and reviews, so we were fishing out of the same pond. And I still had to pay for it.

The publicist went to blogs outside of my book's genre. They found a handful of bloggers who would review my book. The worst reviews I received were through the people invited by the publicist. This was because they were reaching out to people outside of my genre. Not a good option. And this was supposed to be a top rated publicist.

Once again, if you are someone who does not want to market yourself, a publicist may be a good option. Keep in mind that in most cases, you will pay more for the service than you'll reap from the publicity. If you are willing to reach out to bloggers that have a readership that likes your type of book, save your money and do your own legwork. Joining a writers group that has a wide diversity of bloggers is a great option. Paying for memberships in professional organizations is a better use of your money.

What is typesetting?

Typesetting is to lay out the chapters, fonts, headings, and justifying the text so that it is readable and professional looking when printed as a book.

Microsoft Word can be frustrating. I know. That's stating the obvious, but how much more true this is when formatting headers and footers. I decided to write this book because of how difficult it was to find relevant information. It seemed like there were sites that gave partial information or settings for business documents, but I wasn't able to find an easy to follow method for formatting a manuscript for printing.

In the following chapters, I am going to take you step by step through formatting a professional looking manuscript for printing. Then I'll walk you through the print book and ebook publishing process through CreateSpace and KDP (Kindle Direct Publishing). These formatting steps will help your book look good in print, whether you use CreateSpace or other printing companies, such as Lightning Source. We want our book's layout to be indistinguishable from the rest of the industry. A cheap looking book will be treated as such.

There are professional typesetting software applications that are used by industry professionals, but these are very costly and have a learning curve. Some articles I found stated that it is impossible to create a proper manuscript using Word, but this is not the case at all. My first book, I Called Him Dancer, was formatted in Word and people are amazed when they find out it was typeset with this 'inferior' Word program. There are some types of books that don't format well in Word, but for the average book, you can customize a professional looking manuscript that is no different in appearance than a professionally typeset one.

By the end of this book, I will have walked you through typesetting your work from beginning to end. It isn't as difficult as people may think. The problem is that Word isn't intuitive. It's not always apparent where to look for the tools you need for each step in formatting. Once you find the right place to click, the setup is easy.

Free Word Template

The following chapters walk you through configuring your manuscript for publishing, but I also have a word document you can download that has all these steps already applied.

You could copy your book, chapter by chapter, into this document, but it works best if you save this as a template. Begin each manuscript with this, and when you've finished writing, you'll just need to update the title page, table of contents, and add chapter names to each footer.

I recommend going through the full setup process at least once. This will help you to use the template effectively, because you'll understand how to update it.

To add a new chapter, just create a section break and apply the Heading1 to the chapter title. Then unlink the footer from the previous section on both the odd and even pages, and add your chapter title. These are the only changes you'll have to make with this template, providing you keep your book at the standard 6x9 page size.

You can save the file as a template, but this will create a few limitations. I update the **title page**, and the last chapter, 'Other Books by this Author', save it, and then make the file Read Only. This will keep you from accidently overwriting the file.

Open it, then Save As with the title of your book. Microsoft Word (as of this writing) will require you to close the newly saved document and reopen it before you will be able to edit it.

Keep the ISBN number blank as a reminder to add it before publishing. The author gives permission to reuse and customize this file, as long as it is not re-sold as a template.

You can download the template at:
http://www.eddiesnipes.com/ebooks/PublishForFreeBookTemplate.docx

Setting Footers on your manuscript

This topic also applies to setting headers.

When setting up a manuscript, it's usually necessary to have the footer change for each section. At a minimum, you want to have a separate footer that begins at the first chapter. You do not want the title page (or pages) to have numbers and footer information. It makes the manuscript look unprofessional.

Let me first define headers and footers. If you're new to Word, this may not be familiar to you. A header is the information printed in the margins at the top of the page, and a footer is the information printed at the bottom of the page. Normally, this information will contain the page number and the chapter title. Some books may also include the book title. In this book, I'll be using the footer since this is the format I prefer, but the exact same methods apply to headers.

Planning your footers.

Decide how you want your footers to display. If you want the same footer throughout the book, you will only need two sections. One for the title page and table of contents, and one for the rest of the book. If you want to have a footer that is unique for each chapter, you'll need to create section breaks at the end of each chapter. This will make the next chapter part of a new section.

To create a section break, go to the end of the last sentence, or the beginning of the title of the next chapter. Click on the Page Layout Tab, click Breaks, then choose Next Page in the section break option. See below:

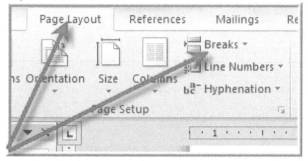

Adding Breaks to Quick Access

Here is a helpful tip. Page breaks and Section breaks are two of the tools you'll use quite often in formatting your manuscript. You'll save a lot of time by adding these two options to your quick access menu.

Right-click on any menu option on the quick access tools, and click on **Customize Quick Access Toolbar**. This process works with most newer versions of word.

Click the down arrow beside **Choose Commands From**, and change it to **All Commands**.

Commands are alphabetical, but not consistent. Section break is not in the 'S' section. It's in the 'I's. Look for **Insert Section Break**. Click it, and click **Add**.

Page break can be added two ways. Go to 'B' and look for **Break**, or to have a drop down of all the break types, look for **Insert Page and Section Break** from the 'I' section again. I prefer the Break tool.

A section break is an invisible field and will act the same as a standard page break. You can see what these breaks look like by revealing the formatting. To do this, click on the paragraph symbol on the home tab in the **Paragraph** section of the tool ribbon.

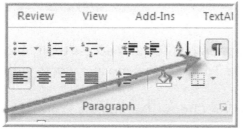

When formatting is revealed, there are few symbols that will help you identify your formatting.A carriage return will start a new paragraph. A line return will not.

Text·with·a·carriage·return·(enter·key)¶
Text·with·a·line·break·(Shift·Enter)↵
Text·after·the·line·break¶
Text·after·the·carriage·return.|¶
¶

There will be times when you'll want to start a new line without starting a new paragraph. Shift-Enter will drop down one line, but will not break the text into a new paragraph. This will keep text from indenting if you have indented paragraphes, such as I am using here.

Word's reveal formatting allows you to identify whether a document is using page breaks or section breaks.

The paragraph symbol indicates a carriage return. The dotted lines indicate a section break. A page break will be symbolized with a single dotted line.

A **page break** serves just as the name indicates. It forces a new page so that the next line of text begins on a new page. The **section break** will also create a new page, but it treats each page within the section as a logically separated block of text. A page break does not create a new section, so any header or footer change will affect the entire section, regardless of how many page breaks there are.

To the reader, these two options don't look different, but when it comes to formatting, section breaks serve a very important function.

If you want to turn off the format reveal, click the paragraph symbol again.

Customizing unique footers for each section.

By default, if you create a footer, the same footer will show throughout your document. So if you put 'Chapter 1' in the footer of your section, the footer on the last page will still say 'Chapter 1', regardless of what chapter you're in. To separate chapters, you'll need to break the link between sections.

To break the section link, go into the footer editing mode. The easiest way to get into editing mode is to move your curser into the margin at the bottom of your page and double click. You will see something like this:

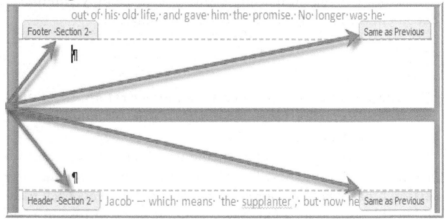

The tab indicates which section you are in. If you have a title page, it should be section 1. Chapter 1 will be section 2, and so on.

Take note of the right-hand tab. This lets you know that this header or footer will pull its information from the previous section. Since this is Section 2, anything in footer of section 1 will show up in these fields.

If section 1 is the title page, you want it to be blank. This makes section 2 blank. However, if you break the link between sections 1 and 2 and put information in the footer, such as 'Chapter 1', then Section 3 will also hold this same information.

If you're going to have a customized formating, such as the chapter name and page number, I recommend customizing the first chapter, and then break the sections up. This way you'll only have to rename each chapter and won't have to customize the formatting and numbers from scratch for each chapter. This will all make sense when we start editing the footers.

Let's begin by breaking the link between Section 2 from Section 1. Section 1 is the title pages, so it won't have numbering or footers. We want it to be blank.

While in the footer editing mode, look at the top of the screen. You should already be under the tab titled 'Design'. See below:

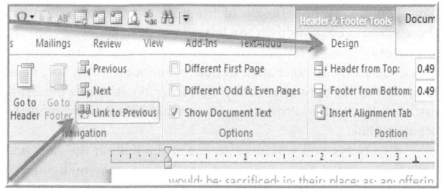

If you don't see this, make sure you are in the footer editing mode by doubl-clicking near the bottom of the page.

To break the link between your current section and the previous section, click on the highlighted area as shown above, **Link to Previous**. This will break your link from section 1 to section 2, but anything below section 2 will remain linked.

Once you click to break the link, the **Same as Previous** tab will disappear from the box around the footer. Also, the highlight around **Link to Previous** will disappear. Now we are ready to format our chapter footers.

In this example, I'm going to use my chapter names and add page numbers. In order to look more professional, I want my even numbers to appear on the left of the page, and my odd numbers to appear on the right. This will make the printed page number to always be on the outside edge of the book for easy viewing. We don't want the numbers to be near the binding where they are hard to see.

In the image above, there is a checkbox that says, **Different Odd and Even pages**. Click to check this option. Your footer banner will change to indicate whether you are on an odd or even page. My first chapter begins on an even page, so I want my page number to be on the left.

Since the book cover isn't considered a page, page 1, an odd number, will begin to your right. This would mean that all odd pages should have the numbers on the right side of the page, so they are closest to the edge where the reader will be looking. Even pages will be on the left side of the book, so the page numbers should always be printed on the left side of even pages.

Note: Some versions of word will re-enable the link to previous section if you change to odd/even footers. You may need to break the link between section 1 and 2 again. It's not a big issue. Just click the 'Link to Previous' option again when you're ready to break the link.

Also Note: You will need to break the link on the first odd page footer in the new section you are editing, *and* you'll need to break the link to previous on the first even page in the section you are editing. If you forget to break the link *before* making changes, you'll have to go back and edit the previous section again. Whatever you type into the footer will populate all the footers in that section, as well as for all linked sections. The same is true for headers.

We are on an even page, so the cursor should be on the left side of the footer. If not, under the design tab, click on **Insert Alignment** and choose **Left**.

Next, insert a page number. Click on the page number icon on the upper right of your menu (see below).

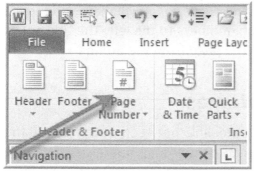

From the drop-down option, select **Current Position**. This will put the page number where your cursor is and make formatting much easier.

I like simple numbers, so I clicked on plain number.

The next thing I want is for my chapter name to appear on the right side of the page. To do this, click on Insert **Alignment option** – see below:

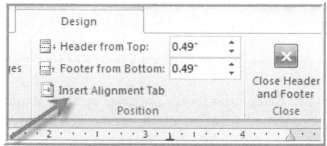

Choose **Right** and click **OK**.

This moves your cursor to the right of the field.

Type in any text you like. Since I want the chapter name to appear, I'll be typing in the title of each chapter.

Now all your even pages should have footers, but your odd pages will have blank footers. If you didn't select the option to have different odd and even pages, then all your footers will be populated with the same formatting and position.

To populate the odd footers, follow the same process as with the even footers, but insert the title first, move the cursor to the right and insert the page number.

<u>Be sure and choose Current Position when selecting a page number option.</u>

Now if you scroll down, each page will have odd page numbers to the right and even numbers to the left. The title needs to be on the opposite side of the page from the numbers.

Changing Chapter Names.

Since we didn't break the link between sections, all the sections will have the correct numbering, but also the same chapter name. This creates a template for your chapters, but you'll need to change the chapter names. This will be quick now that you have completed your formatting. The first step is to break the link between sections.

Move to the next chapter and go into the footer. If the section number doesn't change, then you haven't created a section break for that chapter. Be aware that if you make a change anywhere in a section, every page will be altered. That means if you are missing a section break and you edit the footer, you will have to go back and fix it after adding a section break.

If you see the tab, 'Same as Previous', Click on the option 'Link to Previous' to break it.

You only have to change the footer once per section. When you make a change to the even pages, all the even pages below it will be changed. The same is true for odd pages.

Do this for each chapter and your manuscript will have a professional style footing that will help readers find the right page and know what chapter they are in. Some authors like to put the title of the book in the header. The process for formatting the header is the same as the footer.

If you've followed these steps, the title page will not have a footer, and each page thereafter will be properly formatted.

Text Formatting

Configuring Word

Before formatting the text, it's important to configure Word with only the features necessary for your book. Fortunately, with word, you can make as many changes as you want and have them ONLY apply to the document you are using. When making a change in Options, you'll see something like the image below:

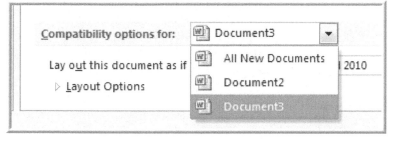

> **Note:** *This applies to Word 2010 and earlier. In Word 2013, this change is unnecessary. When you open an older file, Word converts it to a 2013 version, and you then must select Save As, then choose an older version if needed. Word 2013 users can skip down to Other Configurations.*

If you click the down arrow, you'll see a list of documents you can make changes to. I have two new documents open. I can apply my change to my current document (which is the default action), another open document, or I can apply this to all new documents. If you are making a change that you want to always be in effect, change to **All New Documents**.

One thing I highly recommend is to strip away all downward compatibility options. To do this, go to File, Options, click advanced, and scroll down to compatibility options. Click the **Lay out as if created in**: and choose the version of word you are using.

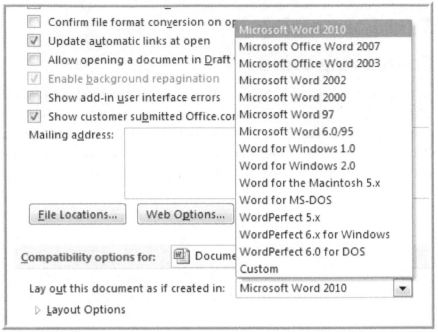

The downward compatibility options enables features that allows your document to be functional in an older version of Word. This won't be necessary for typesetting. The finished product will be saved as an Adobe PDF document, so there will be no need for compatibility with other word processing applications. Changing this to your current version of Word will keep *downward compatibility* from interfering with your formatting.

To make a book printed page look good, the text will have to be justified. Word has a tendency of stretching the text when trying to fill up a line. Though newer versions have improved in this area, the Word Perfect Style of justification is much better for typesetting. Word allows this option, but it is buried out of site. To enable **Word Perfect justification**, click on File, Click Options, then click Advanced. Scroll to the very bottom and you'll see Compatibility Options.

> **Note**: *This also is not available in Word 2013, so this step is unnecessary for 2013 users.*

Click the arrow to expand in order to reveal the various setting options. Scroll to the 'D's' and you'll see '**Do full justification**

the way WordPerfect 6.x for Windows does'. Check this option as shown below:

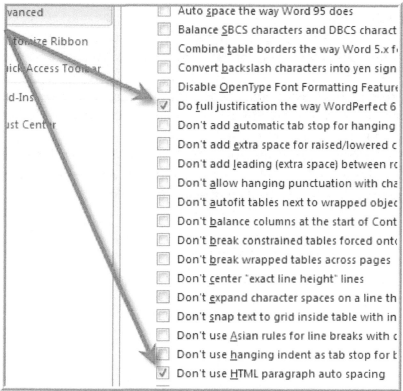

While you're in this area, also check the box, 'Don't use HTML paragraph auto spacing'. This formatting option can produce unexpected results.

One last option you should turn off is, 'Use Printer Metrics to layout document.' Uncheck this box. This option can alter the layout based on the printer's driver your computer uses. Since this is not going to be printed with a personal computer, this should not be used. It can cause the document to look one way on your computer, but different when printed in book format.

From this point on, formatting is an easy task.

Other configurations

Embedding Fonts

It's always a good idea to embed the fonts you are using when preparing a document for printing. If the font is not embedded, the publisher will substitute the closest compatible font, but this can alter the look of your manuscript. Embedding will avoid this problem. I'll mention this later when it's time to create the pdf, but let's get familiarized with this now.

To embed, click on file, options, Save and then scroll to the bottom of the window. Below '**Preserve fidelity when sharing this document**', click **Embed fonts in the file**. See below:

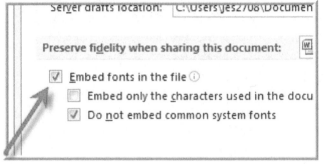

Embedding fonts greatly enlarges the file size, so to save space, you may want to check the option to not embed common system fonts. It also won't hurt to leave this unchecked. By default, this action is only applied to the current document you have active. If you want to apply this to all Word documents, click the drop down arrow and choose All New Documents. This will increase the file size of all your word documents, but in the era of large hard drives, this may be worth enabling so you don't forget to enable it in the future.

When you go to save the manuscript as a PDF file, DO NOT print to a PDF file. This will not preserve your fonts. Instead, click on File, Save As, and choose .pdf as your file type.

Formatting the text

Depending on how you put your book together, you might have various fonts. I cut and paste from another application, and sometimes it creates a mixture of fonts. Try not to have more than one font in your final document. In rare cases, you may want to use a second one, but the less fonts the better.

To make sure your entire document has only one style of font, follow these steps.

Press Ctrl-A. This will highlight all the text in the document.

Now select a font. Choose a font that looks good in print. Times New Roman isn't as readable in book format as some of the other fonts. I prefer Calibri or Century Schoolbook. These format well and look good in print, but feel free to use what fits your book.

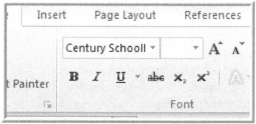

Leave the font size blank. This is important because any headings or formatted text will be changed and will produce unexpected results. If you have mixed font sizes, you may have to manually change them where needed.

Aligning the Title Page

The title page should be centered. Press Ctrl-Home. This will take your cursor to the very top of the document. Hold down the shift key and press the down arrow. Press it until you get to the bottom of the title page.

With the text highlighted, Click the Center Alignment icon. You can find this on the Home tab on the Word menu. See Below:

Justifying the Body.

Move your cursor to the beginning of chapter 1. Make sure the cursor is in front of the first letter of text. See below:

Simple·Faith¶

The·Apostle·Paul·wrote·to·the·Corinthian·church·and· expressed·his·fear·that·they·might·be·drifting·away·from·the· simplicity·of·their·faith·in·Christ.·The·same·threat·faces·you,·your· church,·and·every·Christian·on·a·daily·basis.·If·we·allow·human· philosophy·to·muddy·the·waters·of·truth,·nothing·will·be·clear.¶
I·once·had·a·discussion·with·someone·about·faith.·In·our· talk,·it·was·stated·that·faith·was·too·complicated·to·understand.· Books·on·theology·and·Christian·philosophy·clouded·the·issue·and· made·things·seem·too·hard·to·grasp·by·anyone·other·than·learned· scholars.·Once·again,·I·pointed·back·to·the·simplicity·of·the· gospel.·The·Bible·says,·"Abraham·believed·God,·and·his·faith·was· accounted·to·him·for·righteousness."¶

Now hold down the Shift and Control keys and while holding, press the key labelled 'End'. This will highlight all the text from your cursor until the end of the manuscript. Now press the Justify icon.

This will justify the text throughout your document and should look something like the image below:

Simple·Faith¶

The· Apostle· Paul· wrote· to· the· Corinthian· church· and· expressed· his· fear· that· they· might· be· drifting· away· from· the· simplicity·of·their·faith·in·Christ.·The·same·threat·faces·you,·your· church,· and· every· Christian· on· a· daily· basis.· If· we· allow· human· philosophy· to·muddy·the·waters·of·truth,·nothing·will·be·clear.¶

I· once· had· a· discussion· with· someone· about· faith.· In· our· talk,· it· was· stated· that· faith· was· too· complicated·to·understand.· Books·on·theology·and·Christian·philosophy·clouded·the·issue·and· made·things·seem·too·hard·to·grasp·by·anyone·other·than·learned· scholars.· Once· again,· I· pointed· back· to· the· simplicity· of· the· gospel·.The·Bible·says·"Abraham·believed·God·,and·his·faith·was·

The jagged look of the text has been replaced with neatly aligned paragraphs.

The paragraph symbol at the end of my paragraphs are from the formatting codes. They will not print and can be turned on or off by clicking the paragraph symbol on the main tab of the Word menu.

To verify that the paragraphs look good, browse through your manuscript and look for any stretched out text. Odd looking paragraphs can be resolved by hyphinating words, adding or subtracting a word, or tweaking the text. Small blocks of indented text, such as quotes, can misformat. It might be helpful to leave these unjustified. To remove justification, highlight only the text that needs adjusting, and click the left alignment icon.

You'll need to play around to resolve any issues, though there should be few – if any. In versions of Word prior to 2013, turning on the Word Perfect formatting resolves most odd paragraphs.

If you have a word that is too stretched out, or several lines that are stretched, you can manually tweak the justification. To do this, highlight the text you want to adjust. Under the Home tab, click to expand the Font options, go to the Advanced tab, and choose to condense the text. See below:

If you're trying to fill in a little text, you can also expand a word or block of text. Some or all of the text can be returned to normal if it looks odd. If your manuscript has an index or other addition at the end of the book, you may want to leave these out of your justification and align them separately.

Any paragraph titles that are stretched can be fixed by highlighting and clicking the Left Justify icon.

Once completed, the look and feel of your manuscript text should be book-ready. Now all you need is a good table of contents and to set up the page layout.

Setting the line space after a paragraph

Beginning with Word 2007, Microsoft change their default formatting for paragraphs. Word automatically adds a line between paragraphs. You can turn this off within the document, but the setting will return on the next document. The template I linked to has it turned off, but if you want to permanently disable this 'feature' in Word, here's how to do that.

In Word 2010 and above, begin by clicking the expansion triangle under the styles ribbon at the top of the screen. Then click the **Manage Styles** icon.

Make sure **Normal** is selected, then click **Modify**.

Click the radio button, **New documents based on this template**.

Click **Format**, and select **Paragraph**.

Text Formatting

Go down to the **Spacing** section, change **before** and **after** to 0, and **Line spacing** to **Single**.

Click Ok until you are back to the Word document again.

Word 2007 is a little different. This version isn't accessible for this book, but the steps are the same, though the locations are different.

The default template that comes with Word 2007 (and later) now sets it to double space. You will have to adjust the template if you don't want that to happen.

- In Word 2007, open a new document, go to the "Styles" group on the "Home" tab and locate the "Normal" style.
- Right click on it, and choose "Modify...".
- In the dialog, press the "Format" button and choose "Paragraph...".
- On the "Indents and Spacing" tab, change the value of the "After" field to 0 and click OK once.
- You are now back in the dialog with the "Format" button.

- Find the radio button that says "New documents based on this template" and make sure it is selected.
- Press OK.

From now on, all your documents based on the normal template (which is the default template used when you start a new document) will have no extra space after a paragraph.

Building a Table of Contents

Whether your book is fiction or non-fiction, it needs a table of contents. Aside from the fact that readers need it to locate the chapter they want, a book with a table of contents looks more professional, and readers can browse the contents to get an idea of what to expect from your book.

Word users have an easy path for creating a table of contents, but it does take a little preparation.

Let's first talk about what we expect our table of contents to display. If your book is fiction, most likely the only information needed is the chapter name and page number. If it's non-fiction, you'll need to decide how much information the reader needs in order to find the right chapter and subtopic.

Unless your book is a technical manual, most likely you won't need more than two levels. Beyond two levels, the contents begin to look crowded. If the content of your non-fiction book is well identified by the chapter name, then stick with one level. However, if your topic has a lot of subtopics, give the reader a few levels in which to find the subtopic they want.

For example, suppose your book is on gardening. One chapter may be on vegetables, one on flowers, trees, composting, etc. Under vegetables, having subtopics in the table of contents on potatoes, tomatoes, beans and other plants would be helpful. But having subtopics under beans would be cumbersome. The chapter may have additional subtopics, but the table of contents probably should not. Of course, that's my opinion; other opinions may differ.

Consider these things while planning your table of contents. You'll need to know how much you want to present to the reader in a moment.

Headings

Headings and headers are not the same thing. We looked at headers when looking at the header and footer options. Headings refers to how the text that identifies a body of your document is formatted. Below is a list of common headings:

The Normal option is the main text of a page. Each paragraph you type is normal by default. In this chapter, we'll be focusing on Heading 1 – 3.

A chapter title should always be set to Heading 1. Subtopics should be heading 2 or 3. The lower the number, the larger the text. Below is an example:

Building a TOC

Growing Potatoes → Heading 1 - chapter name

Normal text paragraph

Preparing the soil → Heading 2 - Subtopic

Normal text paragraph

Types of Potatoes → Heading 2 - Subtopic

Normal text paragraph

Sweet Potatoes → Heading 3 - Subtopic of 'Types of Potatoes

Normal text paragraph

Irish Potatoes → Heading 3 - Subtopic of 'Types of Potatoes'

Normal text paragraph

If the above example was the complete content of the book, it would produce one of the following tables of contents:

Contents

The first example creates a table with all three headings. Heading 1 is the chapter, heading 2 is the subtopic under heading 1, and heading 3 is the subtopic under heading 2. Decide which format is best for your book, and choose the depth of your table of contents when you insert it.

When formatting my book, I always use headings to indicate a topic or subtopic – even if I don't plan to use them in a table of contents. I rarely include heading 3 in the TOC, but if I decide it's needed, having headings already in place makes the job a lot easier.

To insert a table of contents, first format all your chapter headings and subtopic headings in your manuscript with the appropriate heading.

Insert a page break right after your title page and make sure the cursor is in that page.

Look at the menu in Word 2010 and click on 'References'. Click on the Table of Contents icon at the upper left. See below:

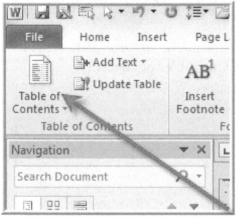

If you plan on using all of your headings in the table, click on **Automatic Table 1**. This will give you a table similar to example 1 above.

If you only want to use heading 1 or 1 and 2, click on '**Insert Table of Contents**' at the bottom of the drop down menu. See below:

Choose the number of levels. See below:

3 will show headings 1 through 3. Choose the level that's the best fit for your book.

Note: If you have trouble finding a heading, you can use a shortcut. For example, if you want to turn a line of text into heading 3, but Word only shows up to heading 2, press **Ctrl-Alt-3**. This will create heading 3 on the line where the cursor is active. This shortcut will also work with heading 1 and 2.

Here is an example from my current book. Since the topics are clear from the chapter titles, I only have one level.

Table of Contents

The Table of Contents is not dynamic, but it can be updated easily. Any time you add text, change the page lay outs, or do anything that might change the page numbers or headings, update the table of contents. Simply put your cursor over the table, right-click, and choose '**Update Field**'. When the window pops up, choose to update the entire table. That way Word will import any headings you have added as well as update the page numbers.

Setting up the Page Layout.

There are a few things to consider when choosing a page layout. The first and most obvious is the size of the book you plan to use. If you are going to be using CreateSpace or Lightning Source, check out the standard layouts they accept. I highly recommend staying with common book sizes. The most common size for most book types is 6x9. That's 6 inches wide by 9 inches long. Most printers (including CreateSpace and Lightning Source) accept 6x9 books.

Click on the Page Layout tab on the ribbon. Then click Size, then more paper sizes. Manually enter in 6 for the Width. 9 for the Height. Go to the bottom of the pop out window and click, **Apply to**: Whole Document.

The margin is the next decision you need to make. For the best results, try to stay between 1 inch and ½ an inch. I prefer to use ¾ of an inch (0.75) for my margins. This allows me to print my header at ½ an inch and maintain a nice look.

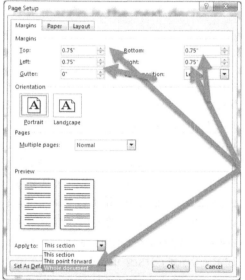

Click on Margin, then Custom Margin.

The header and footer text will print outside of the main text area, so these margins must be smaller than the text margins. For example, if you set your page margins for .75, then you will need your header and footer margins to be smaller. Maybe something like .5. If they were the same setting, the footer would print on top of the page text. If they are too close, it will look like a misprint or part of the page text. I recommend keeping the headers and footers at least .25 (1/4 of an inch) away from the page margin.

If a margin page is too narrow, the printed text will show up in the gutter of the book. This is the area near the book's binding.

Setting each area as .75 is a good starting point. Be sure and change Apply to: Whole Document. Click on the Layout Tab.

Set Header and Footer to .05. This can be adjusted if it doesn't look right for your book layout. Again, make sure Apply to is changed to Whole Document.

Line Spacing

When submitting a manuscript to agents or editors, the standard formatting is double-spaced lines. This may be the standard for evaluating manuscripts, but it is not the standard for printing a book. Double-spaced lines do not look good in print.

There are a lot of line spacing options, but this instruction is intended as a quick reference for the most common book types. I recommend changing the line spacing to 1.0. If the lines look crunched together, you can manually set it to 1.15 or something similar. To set this option, highlight the entire document, or if you want to exclude the title page, place your cursor in front of the first letter of chapter one, and then press Ctrl-Shift-End. This will take you to the bottom of the manuscript and highlight all the text from chapter one until the end.

From the Home tab, click on the drop-down arrow beside the line spacing icon. See below:

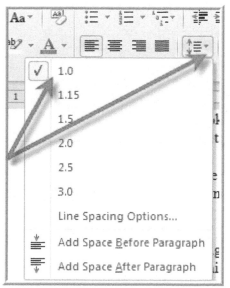

1.0 looks good for most books. You can also click Line Spacing Options and manually adjust it to your liking.

Orphans

An orphan is a word or line of text that is left hanging by itself. In a printed book, this can be very unattractive. You don't want to have the last few words of a chapter sitting alone on a page. Usually orphan control is enabled by default, but to make sure it's turned on, do the following.

Place your cursor anywhere in a body of a normal text paragraph. Make sure the Home tab is selected, and click the expansion button under Paragraph. See below:

Go to the Line and Page Breaks tab and make sure the Window/Orphan Control is checked.

Publishing on Create Space

I recommend publishing the print book before the ebook. It takes longer to get the print book setup, but it provides you with a ready to publish cover when you are done, and it auto-links the ebook to the print book if you follow these steps.

Before You Publish

Prior to publishing, you'll need to create new accounts on Kindle and CreateSpace. For Kindle, go to http://kdp.amazon.com

Amazon walks you through the setup, so I won't cover that here. Once you are setup, go to http://www.createspace.com. Again, you'll have to follow the new account setup process and set up banking information to handle the royalty payments you'll receive from your mega bestseller book.

If you are planning to create your own book cover, or have the book cover designed for you, download the template before you start a CreatSpace project. If you plan to use the CreateSpace cover design tool, you can proceed with your book publication. To design a cover, skip ahead to the Design a Cover chapter of this book. If you are reading this in an ebook, click here.

Begin Your Project

At this point, you should already have the manuscript PDF ready for upload. If you are not using the cover creator on CreateSpace, you should also have a PDF file for the completed book cover.

If you are not already there, in your web browser, click on Member Dashboard. Then click on Add New Title.

Put in a Title for your project. This does not have to be an exact match for your book title. It's for your reference. It's the title name you will see as a link in your Member Dashboard. Select Paperback, then click on Get Started by the Guided step by step option.

The next page is where you have to put in the title as you want it to appear on your book. If your title or author name is not an exact match to what is in your manuscript, you'll get an error during the review process and you'll have to fix it.

The options with the red asterisks(*) are required. The subtitle is optional, but I highly recommend you take advantage of it. This will be included in the keywords that will show up when visitors are searching Amazon. Some authors pack the subtitle with keywords. Others, like myself, just try to have a relevant subtitle that helps define the content of the book.

Primary Author is required. If you have a co-author, you can click **Add** and include them in the book information.

Series Title If you are publishing a book that is in a series, check the 'This book is part of a series' option, and include the **Series Title.**

You can choose a publication date from Today's date and earlier. You don't have the option to future date a publication.

Click **Save and Continue.**

Now is a moment of decision. You have the four options below:

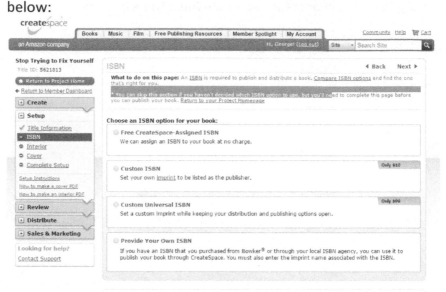

What is an ISBN? An ISBN number is the numbering standard booksellers and distributors use to order books from publishers. All ISBN numbers link back to a database at Bowker (bowker.com). In the past, publishers (including independent authors) had to go to myidentifiers.com, create an account, and purchase ISBN numbers.

They would then register their publishing imprint as the publisher of record, and assign ISBNs to each book along with author info, a book cover image, and a description. The cost for a single ISBN number is $125. As of this publishing, a bulk purchase of 10 numbers is $295. The price per number goes down based on the amount of bulk purchase.

Amazon has changed this. Their combined bulk purchasing power has made ISBN numbers available to authors for $10, if you want to set up your own imprint as the publisher of record, or free if you want CreateSpace to be the publisher of record.

Four ISBN Options

The **Free CreateSpace-Assigned Option**. If you don't care if your book is listed in Bowker with CreateSpace as the publisher, you can choose this option for no cost. Amazon will assign an ISBN number to your book from their own bulk of numbers. Keep in mind that this number can never be changed. Your book will forever be listed as published by CreateSpace in any lookup by a reseller.

Custom ISBN. This gives you the option to user your own Bowker account to purchase an ISBN, but get the price at Amazon's $10 rate. If you don't yet have an account, you can create one at myidentifiers.com, and login through this CreateSpace interface and get the discount.

This will make your own imprint the publisher of record. For example, for my publishing, instead of my books showing up as 'Published by CreateSpace', they will show up as 'Published by Exchanged Life Discipleship.' In the case of this book, since it is solely for Amazon related publishing, I would save $10 and choose the free option.

Custom Universal ISBN gives you the opportunity to keep your options open for the future. For a $99 fee, you can use a universal ISBN than can be ported to a different publisher. It would be rare to need this option.

Provide Your Own ISBN. If you already have ISBN numbers you have purchased, you can choose this option, and then assign one of your own numbers to your book. You would have to log on to myidentifiers.com and manually assign the number to your book as well. Otherwise, you would have incomplete information on the Bowker database.

For this example, I'm selecting the option to publish with a **Custom ISBN**. This prompts for the myidentifiers.com username and password.

The user is prompted to confirm their imprint name. If someone has multiple imprints under their account, there will be an option for each imprint name.

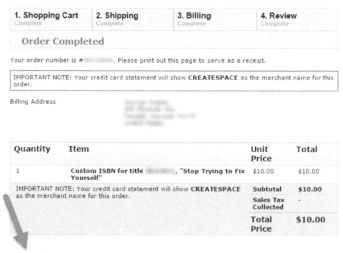

Once completed, you'll get a message indicating that CreateSpace
will be the merchant that shows up on your bank statement for
the purchase of the $10 ISBN.

Below is the ISBN that has been assigned to the book. The below numbers can be given to any retailer that can purchase from Ingram or Amazon, and this book will be available for order. Of course, it takes a few weeks for this to replicate into all retail databases.

Copy the ISBN-13 number and past it into your manuscript.

A·book·by:¶

Exchanged·Life·Discipleship¶

¶

¶

¶

Save the document as a word document for your backup. Save it again as a .PDF document. If you followed the manuscript process in this book, your fonts should already be embedded. This will insure your book will print correctly, even if the printer does not have that font installed.

When saving the .PDF file, follow these steps:

- Add the date at the end of your file name. This will help you identify the right file if you have to make a change and upload again.
- Select Standard as the optimization.
- Click Options
- Select ISO 19005-1 Compliant PDF/A
- Click OK
- Save to a location where you can easily locate it. It's recommended that you save the manuscript word doc, cover design files, book cover pdf, and manuscript pdf in the same folder. This will keep things organized and make your life a lot easier.
- Once saved, go back to CreateSpace and click Continue.

The next page gives several options. If your book has only black and white, click that as the **Interior Type**. If your book has color photos, or illustrations that need color, you'll need to select full color. This will increase the print price of your book.

The **paper color** is either white, or cream – which is an off white. Most books don't look good with Cream, so white is the normal default.

The **Trim Size** is the dimensions of your book. The standard size for most books is 6x9. Unless you have a good reason to change it, I recommend staying with the standard. If you want a different size, click on **Choose a different size** and select it. Keep in mind that your trim size must match your page setup in your manuscript and book cover size you created.

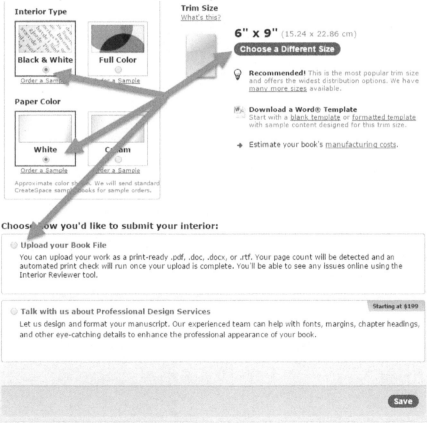

Select **Upload your Book File**.

This will give you another couple of options.

Click browse and select your manuscript PDF.

> • For the **Bleed** option, you'll almost always select 'Ends before the edge of the page.' A text book wouldn't want to bleed text over the edge of the page.
>
> • It's recommended that you check the box for 'Run Automated Print Checks'. We'll see the results of this shortly.
>
> • Click Save at the bottom of the page, and the file will begin uploading. Your internet speed will determine how long this will take, but the manuscript upload usually isn't very long.

Once the upload is complete, you'll get this message:

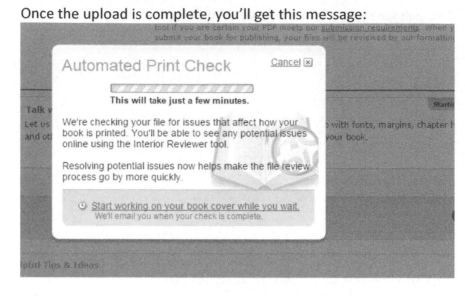

Once you are used to working with CreateSpace, you can click on 'Start working on your book cover' and come back to the check later. In this book, we'll stay in order.

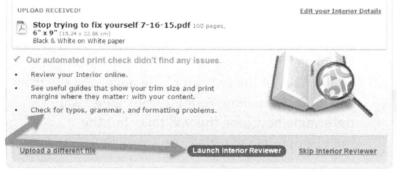

If an error is found by the automated process, it will show up here. Then you can review the error and decide if the original manuscript need to be fixed and uploaded again.

Click 'Launch Interior Reviewer.

It may take a few minutes to load. Once loaded, it will give you a virtual view of your book. Check the page number format to make sure the numbers are at the edge of your book, and make sure the footers and page edges are correct and within the dotted lines.

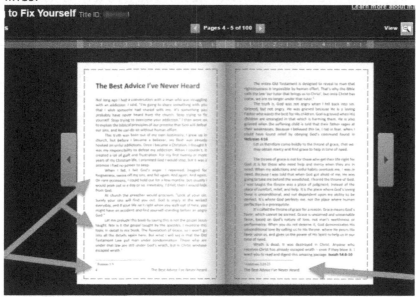

Another important thing go check is the table of contents. Verify the number on your TOC matches the page number in the viewer. You can jump to a page by typing it in at the top and clicking 'Go'.

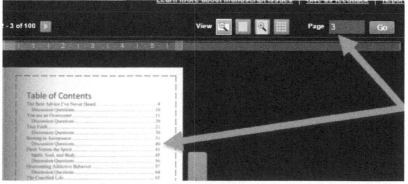

Once you're satisfied, click on 'Close Interior Reviewer' and this will return you to your project.

You'll be given the option of glossy or a matte finish. Most books are glossy, but if you want a cover that doesn't have a glossy look, matte is an option.

The next choice is to build a cover with the CreateSpace cover creator, hire Create Space to design you a cover, which is fairly expensive, or upload a pdf cover you already designed.

○ **Build Your Cover Online**
Cover Creator is our free online tool for designing a professional-quality book cover using your own photos, logos, and text. This handy tool automatically formats and sizes your cover based on your book's trim size and page count.

○ **Professional Cover Design**   Starting at $399
Work with our expert team to design a standout cover for your book. Select impactful colors, fonts, and images, and use your own back cover text and favorite author photo.

○ **Upload a Print-Ready PDF Cover**
Design your own book cover and format it as a print-ready PDF.

Save

The next chapter goes through the cover design. In this process, I'll continue, assuming you already have a cover ready. To jump ahead to Design A Cover, click here. Then come back to this page when you are ready to upload.

Click the option to Upload a Print-Read PDF Cover, browse to the PDF of your cover, then Click Save.

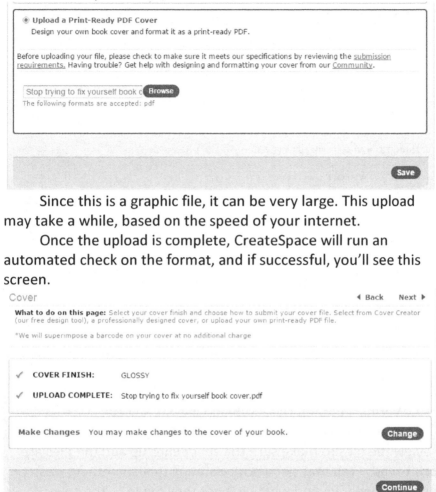

Since this is a graphic file, it can be very large. This upload may take a while, based on the speed of your internet.

Once the upload is complete, CreateSpace will run an automated check on the format, and if successful, you'll see this screen.

When you click Continue, you are given a final verification where you can see the files you uploaded, size of the book, and other information.

Complete Setup

◀ Back   Next ▶

What to do on this page: Review your title setup summary. If all of your information is correct, then submit your files for review. You can edit your book's information before completing the setup of your project. Please note that we will print files exactly as submitted.

Stop Trying to Fix Yourself
Learn to Rest in the Overcoming Power of the Spirit
BY_AUTHOR Eddie Snipes

[Edit]

ISBN-13: 978-0692491874 (Exchanged Life Discipleship)

[Edit]

6" x 9" on WHITE Paper (100 pages, Black & White)
15.24 x 22.86 cm

Interior: Stop trying to fix yourself 7-16-15.pdf

[Edit]

Cover Finish: Glossy
Cover: Stop trying to fix yourself book cover.pdf

[Edit]

By clicking Submit Files for Review, you are agreeing to and confirming your compliance with the Member Agreement

Return to your Project Homepage without completing setup   [Submit Files for Review]

Verify, and then click 'Submit Files for Review.

The review process takes up to 24 hours. A live person will review the files to make sure the cover lines up and the files are print-ready. You may get a notice stating that something wasn't properly lined up, and what changes they made to the cover. CreateSpace will make minor adjustments, but major problems will be rejected.

You can finish setting up your content, but the book will not be publish ready until the review is finished. Until then, you can set up the distribution options and pricing.

Finishing the Book Details

The next option you'll see is the distribution channels.

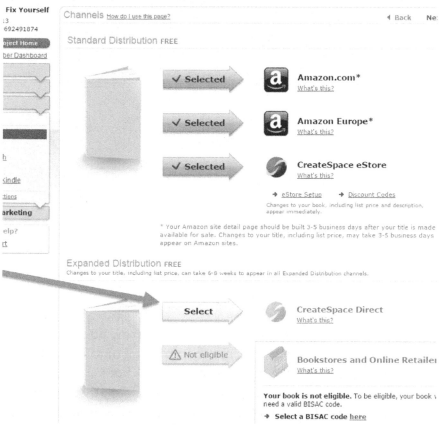

Select CreateSpace direct if you want to have the option to make the book available for direct purchasing. You can set up a storefront where the book can be sold through CreateSpace. Direct sales through CreateSpace give you a higher royalty. You can also set up coupon codes to have sales you can't have through Amazon.

The bookstore option will be available after you finish setting the book up.

Click Save and Continue.

You can set your own pricing. The red arrow points to the minimum allowable price. This number is based on the number of pages and other options you selected for your book.

When you set your price and click 'Calculate', the exchange rate is automatically calculated and other prices in other markets are set. You can override and set the price to what you want, as long as you don't go below the minimum price.

The chart to the right is the estimated royalty payout for each book sold for each market, such as Europe and Great Brittan.

Click Save and Continue.

You'll be prompted again for the cover style, matte or glossy. Unless you've changed your mind, press continue again.

The next screen is the Description information.

Description _{How do I use this page?}

◀ Back   Next ▶

Stop Trying to Fix Yourself
By Eddie Snipes

Description *
What's this?

Maximum 4000 characters - 4000 characters remaining
Advanced users can use limited HTML instead of plain text to style and
format their description

BISAC Category *
What's this?

Choose...

→ Enter a BISAC code

Additional Information (optional)
Add more information about your book, including an author biography, book language, and more, which will appear in certain sales channels.

Author Biography   Add
What's this?

Book Language   English   ▼
What's this?

Country of Publication   United States   ▼
What's this?

Search Keywords
What's this?

Contains Adult Content   ☐
What's this?

Large Print   ☐
What's this?

Save   Save & Continue

Most of this is self-explanatory. For the description, you can cut-n-paste the same information you have on the back of your book, or you can write a different description.

You can add an author bio, by clicking Add.

Put keywords in that you believe will help others find your book. The print book has a maximum of five keywords. When we get to the ebook, you'll have seven keywords. A keyword is anything between the commas. For example, 'Photography' is one keyword. 'Nature Photography' is also one keyword. as long as there isn't a comma between the words.

You have an option to check if your book is large print, and if you are writing garbage, click to indicate it is adult content.

Now let's look at the BISAC category. This is the category your book will show up in retailer databases. You can only select one category, so choose wisely. Your ebook version will have the option of two categories.

Since the book being published here is a Christian book, I've burrowed down to the category that best fits. When you find the right category, click the 'Choose this Category button.

Save and Continue.

This is as far as you can go until the book is approved. I don't recommend working on the Kindle version until the book is approved. If you don't use the 'Publish on Kindle' option you're ebook and print book won't link on Amazon's site without opening a request with their support to link them. Plus, you'll need the Kindle-Ready cover to port into KDP (Kindle Direct Publishing).

I **do not** recommend using the book interior file for the kindle. Your formatting will not be good. Download this as a backup for your manuscript, but do not use it for your kindle book. You can begin preparing your <u>kindle ebook by clicking here</u>.

You can now go back to distribution by clicking 'Channels'. Now you can click on the select button beside 'Bookstores and Online Retailers'.

Expanded Distribution FREE
Changes to your title, including list price, can take 6-8 weeks to appear in all Expanded Distribution channels.

Select → Bookstores and Online Retailers
What's this?

✓ Selected → CreateSpace Direct
What's this?

⚠ Not eligible → Libraries & Academic Institutions
What's this?

Your book is not eligible. Your book must have a

You will notice that your book is not eligible for Libraries and Academic Institutions. To have this option, you must use a CreateSpace assigned ISBN. Since most institutions will not accept self-published work anyway, this does not impact most people.

After Your Book has been Approved

You should get an email stating the book is approved and you need to order a proof copy.

On the dashboard, you'll see 'Awaiting Proof Order' beside the book title. When you click on your book project, you'll see the notification of Proof Your Book.

Any adjustments CreateSpace made to your book will be listed.

The above is a common adjustment CreateSpace makes on book covers. The template isn't always accurate, so minor adjustments have to be made to insure quality printing.

Scroll down to your proofing options.

It is recommended that you order a proof copy before making it available for sale. If you order a proof, the inside first page will have a watermark that says, "Proof Copy." Once you approve, everything will be the same except for the proof notice. Your book will not be available until you approve it. Each proof will be same as the normal author copy price. In this example, the minimum price was $5.38, but the author copy price is $2.15. You can order as many as you want at the lower price, plus the cost of shipping.

Once you are comfortable with the process, you can rely on the digital proof and approve without having to wait for a printed copy to review.

Click on **Digital Proof**.

You have two options. Instead of downloading the digital proof, you can download a clean PDF of the book from the 'Publish on Kindle' screen. The PDF proof file will have extra pages that aren't on the normal PDF file. Click on Launch Digital Proofer.

Look at your book cover. This is what the cover will look like when printed. This proofer tool is almost exactly the same as when you uploaded your manuscript. The only difference is the book cover.

Once you exit the Proofer, scroll down to the approval options.

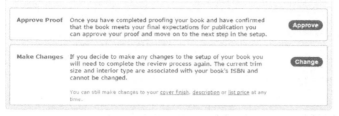

If the digital proofer looks good, you can either approve based on the proof, or wait for a printed copy. If in doubt, order a printed proof.

If you need to make a change, click on 'Change' and upload an updated cover or manuscript. You can also make a change from either the Interior or Cover page. Be aware that once you click on change, you have to resubmit the book for review and wait up to 24 hours again.

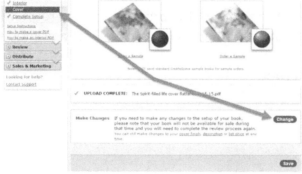

If you click 'Change', you'll get a warning like the one below.

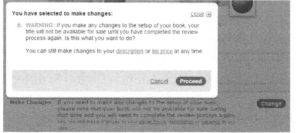

Once you click 'Proceed' your book is listed as waiting approval again and will have to be resubmitted – even if you don't make any changes.

If you want to upload a new cover, select the radio box next to **Upload a Print-Ready PDF Cover** and click the link below your book file name.

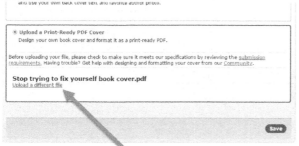

From here, you'll follow the exact same process as when you originally submitted the book.

Once you approve your book, the 'Publish to Kindle' option will become available.

your Amazon account or create a new one.

3 **You'll find your book.**
Your book will be waiting for you in your KDP Bookshelf. Check to make sure everything looks okay before completing the publishing process on KDP.

- Make your book available in more formats so your readers have more choices.
- Reach millions of readers on the Amazon Kindle Store.
- Participate in KDP's 70% royalty program.
- Participate in the Kindle MatchBook program and earn more royalties.
- Publish your work to many countries around the world.

| I want to publish my book on Kindle | No Thanks |

Want to download your book cover and interior files?
Here are the files we'll be sending to KDP - feel free to download them to your computer for safe-keeping.

Kindle-Ready Book Cover
Stop_Trying_to_Fix_Y_Cover_for_Kindle.jpg
⬇ Download Kindle-Ready Book Cover to my computer

Book Interior File
Stop_Trying_to_Fix_Y_Interior_for_Kindle.PDF
⬇ Download this file to my computer

Click to Download the Kindle-Ready book cover. You'll need this for the ebook setup. You can download the book interior file for your own backup, but do not use this for the Kindle ebook. The formatting will leave a lot to be desired.

Now go to the Publish on Kindle chapter. If you are reading this on kindle, click here.

Designing a Cover

There are three options for preparing a book cover. You can hire the work out to a graphic artist, which are plenteous online. If you are looking for a cover, contact me at http://www.eddiesnipes.com and I'll quote you a price. There are a number of designers online. You can hire through CreateSpace, but $399 for a book cover seems a little steep to me.

You can also design your own cover through the cover creator using templates. This option does allow you to upload pictures that you have a license to use, or you can use one of the photos in CreateSpace's templates.

A word of caution. Don't publish without licensing a photo. Many sites don't look kindly on this option.

Cover Creator Online

The online cover creation tool has 30 cover templates (as of this writing).

The templates are not bad, but you have limited control. When you choose a template, it will launch an 11 task workflow.

Choose the theme of the template, click next, and the tool will walk you through each step. You can spend as much or as little time as you want on the cover. Many items can be hidden, such as the subtitle.

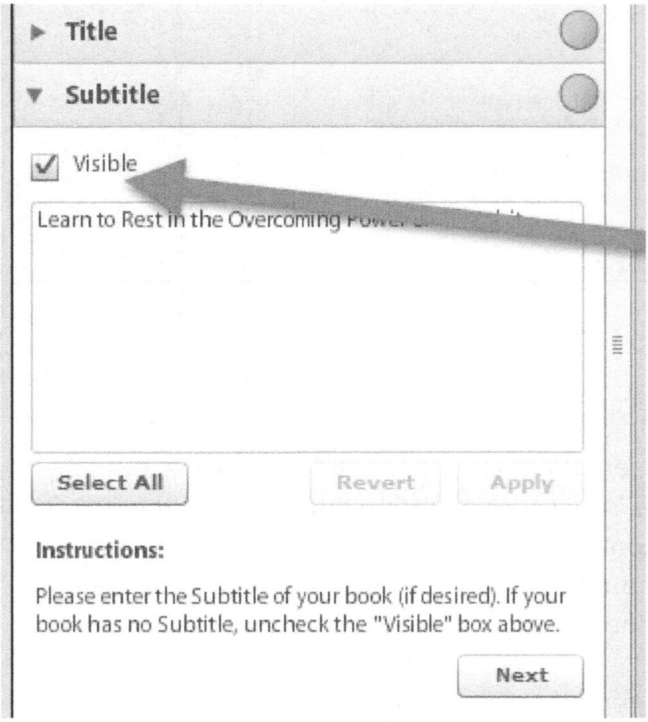

▶ **Title**	◯	
▼ **Subtitle**	◯	

☑ Visible

Learn to Rest in the Overcoming ~~Power~~

| Select All | Revert | Apply |

Instructions:

Please enter the Subtitle of your book (if desired). If your book has no Subtitle, uncheck the "Visible" box above.

| Next |

Uncheck the box and it will be removed from the cover. The cover creator is self-explanatory, so we won't cover each step here.

Some of the down sides are that you can't choose a different font or style that isn't part of the template. For example, in the Chestnut Design I'm using here, the back cover text forces all caps.

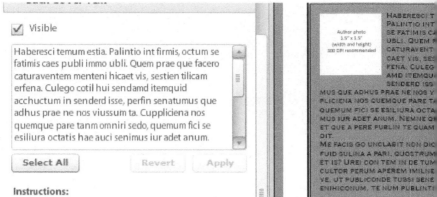

As you can see, the text is upper and lower case, but when it's applied to the back cover, the template converts the text to all uppercase. The tool is good for basic covers, and some cover styles work well. But if you have an idea in mind for your book cover, you may find the cover designer doesn't give you much flexibility.

Book themes work well with the templates in cover creator. I prefer to design covers in Photoshop, but I used the cover creator tool for this book.

Once you click 'Submit Cover', you are back to your project.

Design Your Cover Using the photo Template

As stated earlier, I prefer to download the design template. This template will work with just about any photo editing application. It will be better with one that has layers, but you could use it with an application that does not.

If you don't have Photoshop, here are a couple of free resources you could use for building your cover:

PIXLR Editor - http://pixlr.com/

GIMP – http://gimp.org

There are also photoshop clones that are fairly effective. PhotoLine is a good option. http://www.pl32.com. It costs around $70. It's much cheaper than Photoshop and has less features, but for cover design, it's a decent alternative.

Of course, Adobe Photoshop is one of the best tools available, with many features that make it worth the price. Here is another option. If you are willing to go back to version CS2 of photoshop, Adobe has made the application and the serial numbers available for download. You can download the full version of Photoshop CS2 at:

https://helpx.adobe.com/creative-suite/kb/cs2-product-downloads.html

I must warn you, after you get on the Photoshop train, you'll find yourself wanting to upgrade to get the latest features. For basic book cover designs, CS2 will be more than adequate.

Begin Your Design

Get started by downloading the template at https://www.createspace.com/Help/Book/Artwork.do

The basic Black and White interior template will be sufficient for most projects.

Book Help > Artwork & Templates

We have developed templates to make it easier for you to quickly create print-ready files in graphic design software programs such as Adobe Photoshop® Adobe InDesign®, or any software that will allow you to open a .png or PDF file and save a PDF file.

Product templates are downloadable files that provide information on dimensions, layout and bleed. You can find additional helpful information in ou Submission Requirements.

We recommend that you format your cover with our templates, but understand that you may already have existing artwork for your book. If this is the case please follow our Instructions for Using an Existing Fully Formatted Cover to ensure your existing artwork will work with our system.

Using our templates is simple. Configure and download the template that meets your book's specifications, then follow the instructions below to create you artwork.

Configure your Template

Interior Type	Black and White ▼
Trim Size	6" X 9" ▼
Number of Pages	100
Paper Color	White ▼

Build Template

How to use your Template

1. Open the PDF or PNG file for the Paperback Book Cover Template in your image editing software.

2. Create a new layer in your image editing software. This layer will serve as the design layer.

3. Design your cover in the design layer, using the template PDF or PNG file as the guide layer. The artwork should extend to the outside edge of the template's pink zone to ensure a white border will not exist within the printed work. Do not move the guide layer, as it is properly aligned for our printing specifications.

4. Ensure text and/or images that are intended to be read do not appear in the pink zones of the template.

5. The barcode area is indicated in yellow on the template. Do not place important images or text intending to be read in the barcode location. We suggest filling in this area with your background color or design.

6. Once your design is complete, you will need to turn off the guide layer so that it is not printed on your final product or rejected during the review process. If you are unable to turn off the guide layer, then you will need to format the artwork so that it completely covers the guide layer.

7. Flatten all layers, save the file as a press quality PDF, and upload the file through your CreateSpace account.

To build an effective cover, you need to know your final page count. This affects the width of the binding. Everything else is the same.

Click 'Build Template'.

We have developed templates to make it easier for you to quickly create pri
Adobe InDesign®, or any software that will allow you to open a .png or PDF fi

Product templates are downloadable files that provide information on dime
Submission Requirements.

We recommend that you format your cover with our templates, but understa
please follow our Instructions for Using an Existing Fully Formatted Cover to e

Using our templates is simple. Configure and download the template that me
artwork.

Once you download the file, you'll get a pdf file and a .png file. This is a zip file that can be opened by double-clicking for Windows users, or by downloading 7zip, which is a free program at portableapps.com.

The only file you'll need is the .png file.

This book will not be a course on creating covers, but we'll look at a few important things to note. When you open the file in a photo editor, you'll see the following:

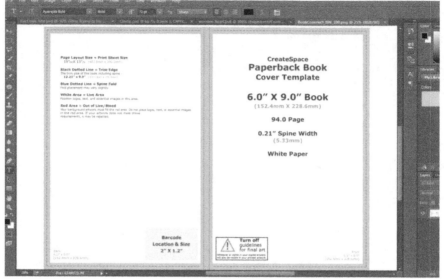

The black dotted lines are the actual book borders. The red lines are the bleed over borders. Trimming a book is not 100% precise, so consider the red areas scrap zones. You want them to be covered with overhang from your cover image so you don't end up with white areas. You don't want key portions of your cover to be in the red zone or it might be trimmed away.

It is perfectly fine if you have pictures or designs in the white areas outside the red lines. This area is neutral space. Anything beyond the red borders will not be included in the book printing. A little overhang is good, because it insures you have adequate coverage up to the edge of the printable area, but if you go too far, it won't cause a problem. Just be aware this won't be part of the printing.

The middle red line is your binding and areas of possible overhang or creasing. If your book is at least 120 pages, you can put a binding title on your book. Otherwise, there isn't enough room to accurately place text on the back binding surface.

Designing a Cover

Below is a mockup of a book cover I'm designing for a book ready for publishing. The image overhang on the right (where it crosses the red border) will be trimmed off in part or completely. The picture of the duct tape crossing into the binding area will print. If there was text here, it could overlap the text. But since this book is too short for a binding title, the overhang will just add to the edge view of the book.

Anything that touches the red area should be something you don't care if it prints or is cut off from the front cover.

The arrow is pointing to the layer that contains the original book cover template file. Once the cover is fully designed, you must turn this layer off. Otherwise, the guides will print on your book.

The yellow Barcode area on the back cover section is an off-limits part of your template. Do not put anything over the barcode. This is how retailers will scan the book at purchase.

When you are placing text on the back of the book cover, which is usually the author's bio and a book blurb, I recommend you uncheck Hyphenate and change the justification to block text, which is in the center of the paragraph options.

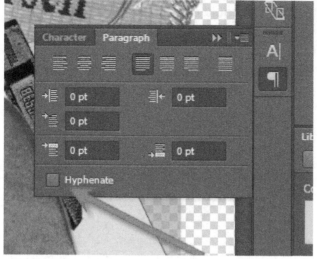

A hyphenated word looks amateurish.

Save often during your design phase. If something goes wrong, it's nice to go back and restore the last successful update.

Once you are satisfied with your book design, save the file as a backup. Then save it again as a PDF file. To do this, click Save As, then click the drop down arrow beside the 'Save as type' option.

Favorites	No items match your search.
Desktop	
Downloads	
Recent Places	
Google Drive	
OneDrive	
Creative Cloud Fi	
Libraries	
Documents	
Music	
Pictures	

File name: Stop trying to fix yourself book cover.pdf

Save as type: Photoshop PDF (*.PDF;*.PDP)

Save Options
Save: ☑ As a Copy
☐ Notes
☐ Alpha Channels
☐ Spot Colors
☐ Layers

Color: ☐ Use Proof Setup:
Working CMYK
☐ ICC Profile: sRGB
IEC61966-2.1
Other: ☐ Thumbnail

Hide Folders   Warning   Save   Cancel

Turn off layers. Some printers require CMYK. Amazon does not accept that color standard. If checked, uncheck the 'Use Proof Setup Working CMYK' box beside Color.

Turn off Layers.

When you click 'Save', you'll get an option box.
• Under General, uncheck everything – including Embed Page Thumbnails and Optimize for Fast Web Preview.
• Change the preset to High Quality Print.
• Click the dropdown arrow, and click 'PDF/X-1a:2001

Save Adobe PDF

Adobe PDF Preset: [High Quality Print] (Modified)

Standard: PDF/X-1a:2001   Compatibility: Acrobat 4 (PDF 1.3)

General
Compression
Output
Security
Summary

General

Description: Use these settings to create Adobe PDF documents for quality printing on desktop printers and proofers. Created PDF documents can be opened with Acrobat and Adobe Reader 5.0 and later.

Options
☐ Preserve Photoshop Editing Capabilities
☐ Embed Page Thumbnails
☐ Optimize for Fast Web Preview
☐ View PDF After Saving

Save Preset...   Save PDF   Cancel

Be sure you don't enable security. Click Save PDF, and save. Your cover is now ready for use on CreateSpace. At this point, go back up to the section on Publishing on CreateSpace to begin your project.

Publishing on Kindle

At this point, you'll need the kindle ready cover (Downloaded from CreateSpace) and the original word document for your manuscript.

Open your manuscript in word, and click on File, Save As.

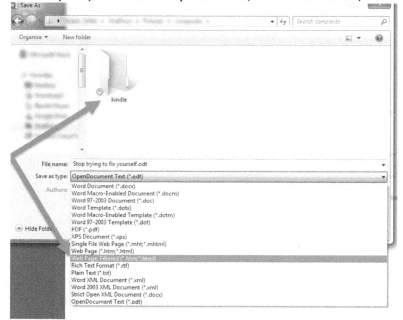

For organizational purposes, create a folder in the same directory as your manuscript and name it Kindle. Open it, and change the file type to Web Page, Filtered *htm, html.

Save the file in the kindle directory.

If you get a warning about some features not being available in that file type, click 'Yes'. The document will change to an html style in word. Your table of contents will change from page numbers to hyperlinks.

Highlight the files in the kindle directory by pressing Cntrl-A. Then Right-Click on one of the files and click Send To, then Click Compressed Zipped Folder.

This will create a new .zip file with the same name as your manuscript file.

You'll upload this file to KDP along with the cover you downloaded from CreateSpace.

It's important to link your ebook and print book properly, so log back into CreateSpace. Click on your book project, then click on 'Publish on Kindle' on the left menu.

Next click on 'I want to publish my book on Kindle'.

your Amazon account or create a new one.

3 **You'll find your book.**
Your book will be waiting for you in your KDP Bookshelf.
Check to make sure everything looks okay before completing
the publishing process on KDP.

- Make your book available in more formats so your readers have more choices.
- Reach millions of readers on the Amazon Kindle Store.
- Participate in KDP's 70% royalty program.
- Participate in the Kindle MatchBook program and earn more royalties.
- Publish your work to many countries around the world.

I want to publish my book on Kindle	No Thanks

Want to download your book cover and interior files?
Here are the files we'll be sending to KDP - feel free to download them to your computer for safe-keeping.

Kindle-Ready Book Cover
Stop_Trying_to_Fix_Y_Cover_for_Kindle.jpg
⬇ Download Kindle-Ready Book Cover to my computer

Book Interior File
Stop_Trying_to_Fix_Y_Interior_for_Kindle.PDF
⬇ Download this file to my computer

Select the option, 'I will upload a separate interior file on KDP, and click Continue.

Publish on Kindle

How would you like us to handle your Interior Book File?

⚠ Your original book file was submitted to CreateSpace as a PDF which is not an optimal format for Kindle. You can transfer your PDF file, but for best results we recommend that you upload a separate interior file on KDP.

○ **Transfer and convert my Createspace interior file.**
You will have the opportunity to preview your converted Kindle book on KDP and upload a new interior file if you desire.

● **I will upload a separate interior file on KDP.**
We will still transfer your Kindle ready cover file and your book title information to KDP.

Continue

You'll be presented with the following options:

Publish on Kindle

Before we can submit your files to KDP, please verify your
Publishing rights and Digital Right Management (DRM).

Publishing rights status: (What's this?)

○ This is a public domain work.

◉ This is not a public domain work and I hold the necessary publishing
rights.

Select a digital right management (DRM) option: (What's this?)

○ Enable digital rights management.

◉ Do not enable digital rights management.

Submit my files to KDP

    Unless you are publishing a fifty year old book as an ebook, you won't likely have a public domain book. This would be a work that can't be copyrighted and is something that is accepted as publically available material. For example, if you decided to publish Shakespeare, that would be public domain. No one has the rights to the work, and no one can publish this as their own work.

    Choose the option that states you hold the necessary publishing rights, which you will if you have written the manuscript and do not have an active contract with another publisher.

    Digital rights is the next option. If you enable digital rights, it encrypts the ebook so it can't be distributed. This also means they can't copy to other devices that can read the Kindle format.

    I prefer not to enable DRM so people who purchase the book can freely use it. The risk of piracy is fairly small. I prefer to make it easier on customers who buy my books.

    Click on '**Submit my Files to Kindle**'.

You'll be prompted to sign into your KDP account. Then most of the book details will be imported from CreateSpace to KDP.

Stop Trying to Fix Yourself	Status	Book Actions
By Eddie Snipes	DRAFT ▾	Continue setup ⋯
	Last modified on July 18, 2015	

When the import is done, it will show in a Draft status, and your cover should show up. If the cover doesn't import as expected, you'll have the option to upload the file you downloaded earlier.

Click **Continue Setup**.

Your first option will be to enroll in KDP Select.

Introducing KDP Select

Take advantage of KDP Select, an optional program that makes your book exclusive to Kindle and eligible for the following benefits:

- **Reach more readers** - With each 90-day enrollment period, your book will appear in Kindle Unlimited in the U.S., U.K., Italy, Spain, Germany, France, Brazil, Mexico and Canada and the Kindle Owners' Lending Library (KOLL) in the U.S. U.K., Germany, France, and Japan which can help readers discover your book.
- **Earn more money** - Earn your share of the KDP Select Global Fund when customers read your books from Kindle Unlimited and the Kindle Owners' Lending Library. Plus, earn 70% royalty for sales to customers in Japan, India, Brazil and Mexico
- **Maximize your sales potential** - Choose from two promotional tools including: Kindle Countdown Deals, time-bound promotional discounts for your book; available on Amazon.com and Amazon.co.uk, while earning royalties; or Free Book Promotion, where readers can get your book free for a limited time.

Learn more

☑ **Enroll this book in KDP Select**
By checking this box, you are enrolling in KDP Select for 90 days. Books enrolled in KDP Select must not be available in digital format on any other platform during their enrollment. If your book is found to be available elsewhere in digital format, it may not be eligible to remain in the program. See the KDP Select Terms and Conditions and KDP Select FAQs for more information.

KDP Select gives the benefits we discussed earlier in this book. It allows your book to be enrolled in the Kindle Lending Library, and it gives you two main promotional options. You can do a countdown sale, where customers see the time clock ticking down until your book goes back to regular price. It also gives you the option to make your book free for up to 5 days during a 90 day period. This is a great way to get your book noticed, and possibly get customer reviews.

There is one main caveat. To enroll in KDP select, you must agree to sell your title exclusively on Amazon for 90 days. You can keep it perpetually enrolled, but each period is for 90 days.

Amazon will crawl the web, and if your book is discovered on another retail site, Amazon will contact you.

Fill in any missing details, such as subtitle, publisher, etc.

3. Target Your Book to Customers

Categories (What's this?)

RELIGION > Christian Life > Personal Growth
RELIGION > Christian Ministry > Counseling & Recovery

Add Categories

Unlike CreateSpace, which is designed to align with the industry print book databases, Kindle allows two categories. Click on Add Categories and find another relevant placement. The more places people can find your book, the better.

Age Range (optional) (What's this?)

Minimum   Maximum
Select ⇕   Select ⇕

U.S. Grade Range (optional) (What's this?)

Minimum   Maximum
Select ⇕   Select ⇕

If you are targeting a specific age or grade, you can select these to match your book's audience. These are optional.

The next option is keywords. Kindle allows two additional keywords. Be sure and take advantage of each keyword, since this will make your book come up more often on searches.

4. Select Your Book Release Option

Please select if you are ready to release your book immediately or if you would like t
(What's this?)

○ I am ready to release my book now
○ Make my book available for pre-order

5. Upload or Create a Book Cover

Upload an existing cover, or design a high-quality cover with Cover Creator. (optional

I have a book cover designed and ready to upload
Please read our Cover guidelines

Browse for image...

I want to design a cover using the Cover Creator (beta).

Launch Cover Creator

The Kindle version allows you to set a release date. Or you can release immediately.

Verify that your book cover image looks correct. If not, click browse for image, and select the cover you downloaded from CreateSpace.

Digital rights should be set to what you selected through CreateSpace. If you changed your mind, you can change it here.

Click Browse to upload your book. Browse to the location where you created the .zip file.

6. Upload Your Book File

Select a digital rights management (DRM) option: (What's this?)

○ Enable digital rights management
○ Do not enable digital rights management

Uploading...

When you click 'Open', it will begin uploading your book.

Once the upload is complete, KDP will convert it to a standard ebook. This can take a few minutes, depending on the size of your book.

> ⟳ Converting book file to Kindle format...
>
> This may take a few moments. If you have completed all required fields above, click "Save and Continue" to move forward while conversion continues.

If you get the below error, save the file again as filtered html, save it to a .zip file, and upload it again.

Book content file:

[Browse]

! We encountered a problem while processing your file. This error may be due to an unsupported or incorrectly formatted file. Please try uploading your book in a different format.

> Learn more about Kindle content creation tools for children's books, educational content, comics and manga.
> Learn KDP content guidelines
> Help with formatting

You'll have a chance to view any spelling errors.
Now you can preview the book, or download it to your local computer for viewing.

Online Previewer

For most users, the online previewer is the best and easiest way to preview your content. The online previewer allows you to preview most books as they will appear on Kindle, Kindle Fire, iPad, and iPhone. If your book is fixed layout (for more information on fixed layout, see the Kindle Publishing Guidelines), the online previewer will display your book as it will appear on Kindle Fire.

[Preview book]

Downloadable Previewer

If you would like to preview your book on Kindle Touch or Kindle DX, you will want to use the downloadable previewer.

Instructions
> Download Book Preview File
> Download HTML
> Download Previewer
  Windows | Mac

Once you click on Preview Book, you'll be prompted to save changes. Obviously, you do want to save.

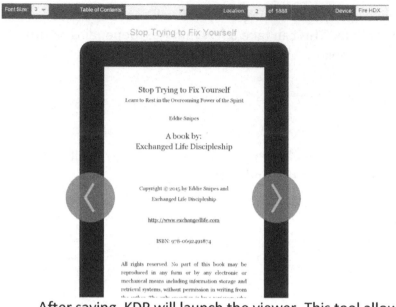

After saving, KDP will launch the viewer. This tool allows you to view your ebook as it will appear in multiple devices. Verify your text looks good, and once you're satisfied, click on **Book Details** at the top left corner of the webpage.

If you're satisfied, click **Save and Continue** at the bottom of the screen.

Unless you intend to limit your book's distribution, go with the default 'World Wide Rights'.

Now you must decide on price and royalty percentage.

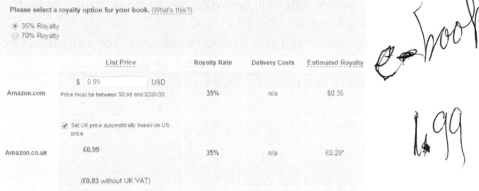

Please select a royalty option for your book. (What's this?)

- 35% Royalty
- 70% Royalty

	List Price	Royalty Rate	Delivery Costs	Estimated Royalty
Amazon.com	$ 0.99 USD Price must be between $0.99 and $200.00.	35%	n/a	$0.35
Amazon.co.uk	☑ Set UK price automatically based on US price £0.99 (£0.83 without UK VAT) ☑ Set DE price automatically based on US price	35%	n/a	£0.29*

If your book is $2.99 or higher, you can choose the 70% royalty option. Unless you feel generous and want to give half your royalties to Amazon, just for the warm fuzzy feelings you get by paying them extra.

If your book is less than $2.99, you have to give up half your royalties and go with the 35% option. The reason for this is that the cost of distribution and system costs has to be made up somewhere. At three dollars, Amazon feels they make enough profit to give the higher royalties.

Going for the $2.99 price seems like a no-brainer, right?

Not exactly. If you are not a big named celebrity, and you are trying to reach a wider audience, a cheaper book may be the way to go. Someone will risk a dollar on an unknown author, but they may not risk three dollars or more.

As of this writing, I've sold over 17,000 books. It's not busting the bank, but the average author sells approximately 70 books. Good marketing and good writing may make you a best seller at full price. Repeat readers will likely be willing to pay $2.99. But new customers won't – at least not for an unknown author.

I have found that my sales increased ten-fold when I dropped my books to .99 cents. This means that even though my royalty percentage is lower, and my revenue per book is lower, I'm still making more than I would have made at $2.99.

I would rather sell more books than to make more money by selling less books. After all, we write because we want people to read our work, right?

This is something you'll need to consider. You can always go back and either raise or lower the book as you see fit.

You have two more options to consider.

10. Kindle MatchBook
☑ This title is enrolled in Kindle MatchBook. Uncheck to opt out of the program

Free   ‡   Estimated royalty $0.00

11. Kindle Book Lending
☑ Allow lending for this book (Details)

☑ By clicking Save and Publish below, I confirm that I have all rights necessary to make the content I am uploading available for marketing, distribution and sale in each territory I have indicated above, and that I am in compliance with the KDP Terms and Conditions.

<< Back to Your Bookshelf   Save and Publish   Save as Draft

The Kindle MatchBook gives you the option to give customers a discounted or free ebook if they have purchased the print version on Amazon. If your book is 99 cents, you can only make it free. If you are 2.99 and over, you can choose the discount. Or you can uncheck the box and make readers buy it again in ebook format if they want it on Kindle.

Finally, you can decide whether or not to include your book in the lending library. I can think of no rational reason to opt out of the lending library. Some months you'll make more royalties from the lending library than from book sales.

The policy of the lending library has recently changed. As it stands today, when someone borrows your book from the library, you get a royalty payment based on how many pages they read.

In the past, payment was given based on how many times a book was borrowed. Authors abused the system by forming borrowing clubs where each person would borrow each others books with no intention of reading it.

To make the royalty system more accurate, Amazon now bases the royalties based on the pages read. When Amazon made this change, they upped the pool of money from 6 million to 11 million. They will calculate the number of read pages from all Kindle online lending library books (KOLL), and divide the money among the authors accordingly.

Decide whether you want extra money or not, then choose to enroll or opt out of the lending library. Now all that's left is to submit the book for publishing. Once you click on Publish, the book is sent to a queue to be reviewed. This can take up to 48 hours, but normally it's between 12 and 24 hours. Until then, you'll see your book in **Review** status.

Once the book is approved, you'll see your status changed to green and Live.

Congratulations! You are now a published author. It can take up to five days for the print book to show up on Amazon, but normally this takes two or three days. It may take up to three more days for the ebook and print version to link on Amazon. When it does, you'll see both editions on the Amazon site, just above the description.

If after three days of being live on Amazon your book is not linked, log in to kdp.amazon.com. Click on help at the top right menu bar, then click **contact us** at the bottom left of your screen. Click on **Publish Your Book** and click in the subject line below the answers to common questions list. Put the subject as 'Need to have ebook and print books linked. In the message, state that it has been over 48 hours and you need your title linked. Give the title, the ASIN of the ebook, and the ISBN of the print book, and send the message.

If you decide to make an audio version, it will also show up as a linked format under your book title.

Promoting your Book

If you opted in to the KDP Select program, you'll see a promo option beside your book at the kdp.amazon.com dashboard.

Status: $0.99 USD   Book Actions:
LIVE ▾   View on Amazon ▾   Promote and advertise   ...
Submitted on January 23, 2014

The ellipsis on the right opens a menu for editing your book options and details. If you click on Promote and Advertise, you'll see the following:

Promote your book on Amazon

Run a Price Promotion

Sign your book up for a Kindle Countdown Deal or a Free Book Promotion. Only one promotion can be enabled per enrollment period.

○ Kindle Countdown Deal Learn more
○ Free Book Promotion Learn more

Create a new Kindle Countdown Deal

Run an Ad Campaign

Advertise your book on Amazon.com. You set the budget, targeting, and timing of your campaign, and you pay only when customers click your ads. Currently Amazon Marketing Services is available only in English. Learn more

Create an ad campaign

Earn royalties from the KDP Select Global Fund

Run an Ad is where you can set up a campaign to pay for advertising on Amazon's sight.

Price Promos gives you two options. You can set up a countdown sale, or you can set up a free promo. If your book is below $2.99, you cannot do a countdown sail, but you can do a free promo.

Create a new Free Book Deal

Choose when the promotion will start and end
Kindle Free Book Deal promotions can run for up to 5 days.

Start Date July 19, 2015   End Date July 21, 2015

Free promotion days used: 3 / 5

Cancel   Save Changes

You have up to 5 free promo days each quarter. You can do five 1 day promos, one 5 day promo, or any combination. Click on the calendar icons and set the date you want the promo to start, and when you want it to end. Click Save, and you're set. You can cancel at any time, or change the dates.

Good luck with your publishing goals. I hope this book has clarified the process and shown that you do not have to pay a vanity press to publish your book for you.

Don't forget to download the free Word template for building your manuscript. The link is:
http://www.eddiesnipes.com/ebooks/PublishForFreeBookTemplate.docx

If you feel this book has saved you money or time, please rate it on Amazon. Thank you!

Other Recent Books by Eddie Snipes

 The Revelation of Grace. The first book in the Founded Upon Grace Series. Discover the biblical truths that explain the defeat of sin, and the unveiling of our position in Christ!

 Stop Trying to Fix Yourself. Why failure is not a barrier to the Christian, and how we can learn to trust in the Spirit's work in our lives, instead of our own. It's time to get beyond feelings of condemnation, and discover what the covenant of promise is about.

 Abounding Grace. Is there such thing as hyper-grace? What does the Bible mean by when it says that the grace of Jesus abounded over the sin that came through Adam.

More books from this author:

- It is Finished! Step out of condemnation and into the completed work of Christ.
- The Victorious Christian Life: Living in Grace and Walking in the Spirit.
- The Promise of a Sound Mind : God's plan for emotional and mental health
- Abounding Grace: Dispelling Myths and Clarifying the Biblical Message of God's Overflowing Grace
- Living in the Spirit: God's Plan for you to Thrive in the Abundant Life

Made in United States
Orlando, FL
23 August 2022

21441557R00059